MY JOURNAL OF FARTS
by

_____

FART GLOSSARY

Amplified Fart: A regular fart done on a metal or hollow surface (like bleachers) will have an exaggerated sound & cool echo.

Command Fart: A fart which can be held in until just the right moment and provide a grand exit from a room upon command.

Cushioned Fart: When a fart is allowed to escape but the butt is strategically pushed down into a soft surface, hoping it will mask all sound and smell until passed. Useful during office meetings or public events.

Organic Fart: A fart by a health food obsessed person who has eaten too much fiber and is proud of their excess gas and uses it as an opportunity to tell you about their natural diet.

Splatter Fart: Oops… you didn't see that one coming.

Squeaker Fart: Anticipating that you have a giant thunder rumble on the way, you release the butt cheeks just a little to allow a small amount of gas to escape and either delay or minimize the huge one on the way.

Balloon Fart: This one is identical to a deflating balloon and is made up of a series of smaller farts which may last an embarrassingly long amount of time. The small scents can combine for a massive stink factor.

Involuntary Fart: You didn't even feel the urge to pass gas but a tiny toot escapes and it's usually followed by a quick throat clearing cough as cover.

Silent But Deadly Fart: The key to this one is that nobody hears anything, but the deadly stench soon suffocates anyone within breathing distance.

Sleeper Fart: Anybody who insists they don't fart will hold it in all day long to prove their point, but when they fall asleep, their body decides it's time to release all of that pressure and it's loud, long and smelly.

Shower Fart: Farts don't smell good as it is, but release one in the shower and that nasty stench will be stuck in your nose for days. Ugh.

A FART BY ANY OTHER NAME...

Enjoy this list of alternative phrases from around the world to describe farts.

After Dinner Mint	Cleft A Boofer
Air Poop	Colon Bowlin'
Anal Salute	Cut The Cheese
Backdoor Trumpet	Heiny Burp
Bakin' Brownies	Let A Beefer
Blow Chocolate Kisses	Poopski
Bottom Burp	Rear Roar
Breaking Wind	Pants Sneeze
Brown Haze	Split The Seam
Butt Yodeling	Strip A Gear
Butt Cheek Squeak	Toot Your Horn
Buttock Bassoon	Back Blast
Butt Burping	Barking Spider
Carpet Creeper	Booty Belch
Extreme Fumagatory Essence	Colonic Calliope
Fanny Bubble	Death Breath
Fire In The Hole	Release The Foghorn
Morning Thunder	Fumigator
Mudslapper	Jockey Burner
Poopy Tunes	Who Let The Beans Out
Puffer	Odor Bubble
Rectal Turbulence	Panty Burp
Ripsnorter	Pop A Fluffie
Scented Scream	Rump Ripper
Stink Sliders	Stink Burger
Sphincter Whistle	Tushy Tickle
Thunder Buns	Turd Tremor
Trouser Cough	Lethal Cloud
Tooshie Belch	Turd Grumble

Date: ___ / ___ / ___   Sun Mon Tue Wed Thu Fri Sat

Time of Fart: _____ am/pm   **Duration:** ___ min ___ sec

Fart Intensity:
- ○ **Gentle Puff** (barely there, quick & unscented)
- ○ **SBD** (silent but deadly)
- ○ **Military March** (series of puffs with mild scent)
- ○ **Classic** (quick, loud, stinky scent but fades quickly)
- ○ **Thunder Rumble** (long, loud & stinky)
- ○ **Diarrhea Storm** (explosive, wet & clears the room)
- ○ **Oh, Crap!** (self explanatory)

Fart Enjoyment Scale: ☺ ☺ ☺ ☺ ☺

Who Noticed: _____

Who Left The Room: _____

Date: ___ / ___ / ___   Sun Mon Tue Wed Thu Fri Sat

Time of Fart: _____ am/pm   **Duration:** ___ min ___ sec

Fart Intensity:
- ○ **Gentle Puff** (barely there, quick & unscented)
- ○ **SBD** (silent but deadly)
- ○ **Military March** (series of puffs with mild scent)
- ○ **Classic** (quick, loud, stinky scent but fades quickly)
- ○ **Thunder Rumble** (long, loud & stinky)
- ○ **Diarrhea Storm** (explosive, wet & clears the room)
- ○ **Oh, Crap!** (self explanatory)

Fart Enjoyment Scale: ☺ ☺ ☺ ☺ ☺

Who Noticed: _____

Who Left The Room: _____

NOTES

NOTES

Date: ___ / ___ / ___   Sun Mon Tue Wed Thu Fri Sat

Time of Fart: _____ am/pm   **Duration:** ___ min ___ sec

Fart Intensity:
- ○ **Gentle Puff** (barely there, quick & unscented)
- ○ **SBD** (silent but deadly)
- ○ **Military March** (series of puffs with mild scent)
- ○ **Classic** (quick, loud, stinky scent but fades quickly)
- ○ **Thunder Rumble** (long, loud & stinky)
- ○ **Diarrhea Storm** (explosive, wet & clears the room)
- ○ **Oh, Crap!** (self explanatory)

Fart Enjoyment Scale: ☺ ☺ ☺ ☺ ☺

Who Noticed: _____

Who Left The Room: _____

Date: ___ / ___ / ___   Sun Mon Tue Wed Thu Fri Sat

Time of Fart: _____ am/pm   **Duration:** ___ min ___ sec

Fart Intensity:
- ○ **Gentle Puff** (barely there, quick & unscented)
- ○ **SBD** (silent but deadly)
- ○ **Military March** (series of puffs with mild scent)
- ○ **Classic** (quick, loud, stinky scent but fades quickly)
- ○ **Thunder Rumble** (long, loud & stinky)
- ○ **Diarrhea Storm** (explosive, wet & clears the room)
- ○ **Oh, Crap!** (self explanatory)

Fart Enjoyment Scale: ☺ ☺ ☺ ☺ ☺

Who Noticed: _____

Who Left The Room: _____

NOTES

NOTES

Date: ___ / ___ / ___   Sun Mon Tue Wed Thu Fri Sat

Time of Fart: _____ am/pm   **Duration:** ___ min ___ sec

Fart Intensity:
- ○ **Gentle Puff** (barely there, quick & unscented)
- ○ **SBD** (silent but deadly)
- ○ **Military March** (series of puffs with mild scent)
- ○ **Classic** (quick, loud, stinky scent but fades quickly)
- ○ **Thunder Rumble** (long, loud & stinky)
- ○ **Diarrhea Storm** (explosive, wet & clears the room)
- ○ **Oh, Crap!** (self explanatory)

Fart Enjoyment Scale: ☺ ☺ ☺ ☺ ☺

Who Noticed: _____

Who Left The Room: _____

Date: ___ / ___ / ___   Sun Mon Tue Wed Thu Fri Sat

Time of Fart: _____ am/pm   **Duration:** ___ min ___ sec

Fart Intensity:
- ○ **Gentle Puff** (barely there, quick & unscented)
- ○ **SBD** (silent but deadly)
- ○ **Military March** (series of puffs with mild scent)
- ○ **Classic** (quick, loud, stinky scent but fades quickly)
- ○ **Thunder Rumble** (long, loud & stinky)
- ○ **Diarrhea Storm** (explosive, wet & clears the room)
- ○ **Oh, Crap!** (self explanatory)

Fart Enjoyment Scale: ☺ ☺ ☺ ☺ ☺

Who Noticed: _____

Who Left The Room: _____

NOTES

_____

_____

_____

_____

_____

_____

_____

_____

_____

_____

NOTES

_____

_____

_____

_____

_____

_____

_____

_____

_____

Date: ___ / ___ / ___   Sun Mon Tue Wed Thu Fri Sat

Time of Fart: _____ am/pm   **Duration:** ___ min ___ sec

Fart Intensity:
- ○ **Gentle Puff** (barely there, quick & unscented)
- ○ **SBD** (silent but deadly)
- ○ **Military March** (series of puffs with mild scent)
- ○ **Classic** (quick, loud, stinky scent but fades quickly)
- ○ **Thunder Rumble** (long, loud & stinky)
- ○ **Diarrhea Storm** (explosive, wet & clears the room)
- ○ **Oh, Crap!** (self explanatory)

Fart Enjoyment Scale: ☺ ☺ ☺ ☺ ☺

Who Noticed: _____

Who Left The Room: _____

Date: ___ / ___ / ___   Sun Mon Tue Wed Thu Fri Sat

Time of Fart: _____ am/pm   **Duration:** ___ min ___ sec

Fart Intensity:
- ○ **Gentle Puff** (barely there, quick & unscented)
- ○ **SBD** (silent but deadly)
- ○ **Military March** (series of puffs with mild scent)
- ○ **Classic** (quick, loud, stinky scent but fades quickly)
- ○ **Thunder Rumble** (long, loud & stinky)
- ○ **Diarrhea Storm** (explosive, wet & clears the room)
- ○ **Oh, Crap!** (self explanatory)

Fart Enjoyment Scale: ☺ ☺ ☺ ☺ ☺

Who Noticed: _____

Who Left The Room: _____

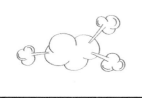

NOTES

NOTES

Date: ___ / ___ / ___   Sun Mon Tue Wed Thu Fri Sat

Time of Fart: _____ am/pm   **Duration:** ___ min ___ sec

Fart Intensity:
- ◯ **Gentle Puff** (barely there, quick & unscented)
- ◯ **SBD** (silent but deadly)
- ◯ **Military March** (series of puffs with mild scent)
- ◯ **Classic** (quick, loud, stinky scent but fades quickly)
- ◯ **Thunder Rumble** (long, loud & stinky)
- ◯ **Diarrhea Storm** (explosive, wet & clears the room)
- ◯ **Oh, Crap!** (self explanatory)

Fart Enjoyment Scale: ☺ ☺ ☺ ☺ ☺

Who Noticed: _____

Who Left The Room: _____

Date: ___ / ___ / ___   Sun Mon Tue Wed Thu Fri Sat

Time of Fart: _____ am/pm   **Duration:** ___ min ___ sec

Fart Intensity:
- ◯ **Gentle Puff** (barely there, quick & unscented)
- ◯ **SBD** (silent but deadly)
- ◯ **Military March** (series of puffs with mild scent)
- ◯ **Classic** (quick, loud, stinky scent but fades quickly)
- ◯ **Thunder Rumble** (long, loud & stinky)
- ◯ **Diarrhea Storm** (explosive, wet & clears the room)
- ◯ **Oh, Crap!** (self explanatory)

Fart Enjoyment Scale: ☺ ☺ ☺ ☺ ☺

Who Noticed: _____

Who Left The Room: _____

NOTES

NOTES

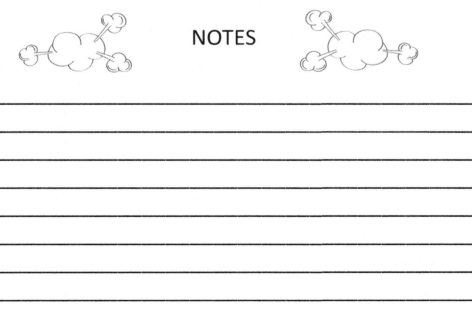

Date: ___ / ___ / ___   Sun Mon Tue Wed Thu Fri Sat

Time of Fart: _____ am/pm   **Duration:** ___ min ___ sec

Fart Intensity:
- ○ **Gentle Puff** (barely there, quick & unscented)
- ○ **SBD** (silent but deadly)
- ○ **Military March** (series of puffs with mild scent)
- ○ **Classic** (quick, loud, stinky scent but fades quickly)
- ○ **Thunder Rumble** (long, loud & stinky)
- ○ **Diarrhea Storm** (explosive, wet & clears the room)
- ○ **Oh, Crap!** (self explanatory)

Fart Enjoyment Scale: ☺ ☺ ☺ ☺ ☺

Who Noticed: _____

Who Left The Room: _____

Date: ___ / ___ / ___   Sun Mon Tue Wed Thu Fri Sat

Time of Fart: _____ am/pm   **Duration:** ___ min ___ sec

Fart Intensity:
- ○ **Gentle Puff** (barely there, quick & unscented)
- ○ **SBD** (silent but deadly)
- ○ **Military March** (series of puffs with mild scent)
- ○ **Classic** (quick, loud, stinky scent but fades quickly)
- ○ **Thunder Rumble** (long, loud & stinky)
- ○ **Diarrhea Storm** (explosive, wet & clears the room)
- ○ **Oh, Crap!** (self explanatory)

Fart Enjoyment Scale: ☺ ☺ ☺ ☺ ☺

Who Noticed: _____

Who Left The Room: _____

NOTES

NOTES

Date: ___ / ___ / ___   Sun Mon Tue Wed Thu Fri Sat

Time of Fart: _____ am/pm   **Duration:** ___ min ___ sec

Fart Intensity:
- ○ **Gentle Puff** (barely there, quick & unscented)
- ○ **SBD** (silent but deadly)
- ○ **Military March** (series of puffs with mild scent)
- ○ **Classic** (quick, loud, stinky scent but fades quickly)
- ○ **Thunder Rumble** (long, loud & stinky)
- ○ **Diarrhea Storm** (explosive, wet & clears the room)
- ○ **Oh, Crap!** (self explanatory)

Fart Enjoyment Scale: ☺ ☺ ☺ ☺ ☺

Who Noticed: _____

Who Left The Room: _____

Date: ___ / ___ / ___   Sun Mon Tue Wed Thu Fri Sat

Time of Fart: _____ am/pm   **Duration:** ___ min ___ sec

Fart Intensity:
- ○ **Gentle Puff** (barely there, quick & unscented)
- ○ **SBD** (silent but deadly)
- ○ **Military March** (series of puffs with mild scent)
- ○ **Classic** (quick, loud, stinky scent but fades quickly)
- ○ **Thunder Rumble** (long, loud & stinky)
- ○ **Diarrhea Storm** (explosive, wet & clears the room)
- ○ **Oh, Crap!** (self explanatory)

Fart Enjoyment Scale: ☺ ☺ ☺ ☺ ☺

Who Noticed: _____

Who Left The Room: _____

NOTES

_____

_____

_____

_____

_____

_____

_____

_____

_____

_____

NOTES

_____

_____

_____

_____

_____

_____

_____

_____

_____

Date: ___ / ___ / ___   Sun Mon Tue Wed Thu Fri Sat

Time of Fart: _____ am/pm   **Duration:** ___ min ___ sec

Fart Intensity:
- ○ **Gentle Puff** (barely there, quick & unscented)
- ○ **SBD** (silent but deadly)
- ○ **Military March** (series of puffs with mild scent)
- ○ **Classic** (quick, loud, stinky scent but fades quickly)
- ○ **Thunder Rumble** (long, loud & stinky)
- ○ **Diarrhea Storm** (explosive, wet & clears the room)
- ○ **Oh, Crap!** (self explanatory)

Fart Enjoyment Scale: ☺ ☺ ☺ ☺ ☺

Who Noticed: _____

Who Left The Room: _____

Date: ___ / ___ / ___   Sun Mon Tue Wed Thu Fri Sat

Time of Fart: _____ am/pm   **Duration:** ___ min ___ sec

Fart Intensity:
- ○ **Gentle Puff** (barely there, quick & unscented)
- ○ **SBD** (silent but deadly)
- ○ **Military March** (series of puffs with mild scent)
- ○ **Classic** (quick, loud, stinky scent but fades quickly)
- ○ **Thunder Rumble** (long, loud & stinky)
- ○ **Diarrhea Storm** (explosive, wet & clears the room)
- ○ **Oh, Crap!** (self explanatory)

Fart Enjoyment Scale: ☺ ☺ ☺ ☺ ☺

Who Noticed: _____

Who Left The Room: _____

NOTES

NOTES

Date: ___ / ___ / ___   Sun Mon Tue Wed Thu Fri Sat

Time of Fart: _____ am/pm   **Duration:** ___ min ___ sec

Fart Intensity:
- ○ **Gentle Puff** (barely there, quick & unscented)
- ○ **SBD** (silent but deadly)
- ○ **Military March** (series of puffs with mild scent)
- ○ **Classic** (quick, loud, stinky scent but fades quickly)
- ○ **Thunder Rumble** (long, loud & stinky)
- ○ **Diarrhea Storm** (explosive, wet & clears the room)
- ○ **Oh, Crap!** (self explanatory)

Fart Enjoyment Scale: ☺ ☺ ☺ ☺ ☺

Who Noticed: _____

Who Left The Room: _____

Date: ___ / ___ / ___   Sun Mon Tue Wed Thu Fri Sat

Time of Fart: _____ am/pm   **Duration:** ___ min ___ sec

Fart Intensity:
- ○ **Gentle Puff** (barely there, quick & unscented)
- ○ **SBD** (silent but deadly)
- ○ **Military March** (series of puffs with mild scent)
- ○ **Classic** (quick, loud, stinky scent but fades quickly)
- ○ **Thunder Rumble** (long, loud & stinky)
- ○ **Diarrhea Storm** (explosive, wet & clears the room)
- ○ **Oh, Crap!** (self explanatory)

Fart Enjoyment Scale: ☺ ☺ ☺ ☺ ☺

Who Noticed: _____

Who Left The Room: _____

NOTES

NOTES

Date: ___ / ___ / ___   Sun Mon Tue Wed Thu Fri Sat

Time of Fart: _____ am/pm   **Duration:** ___ min ___ sec

Fart Intensity:
- ○ **Gentle Puff** (barely there, quick & unscented)
- ○ **SBD** (silent but deadly)
- ○ **Military March** (series of puffs with mild scent)
- ○ **Classic** (quick, loud, stinky scent but fades quickly)
- ○ **Thunder Rumble** (long, loud & stinky)
- ○ **Diarrhea Storm** (explosive, wet & clears the room)
- ○ **Oh, Crap!** (self explanatory)

Fart Enjoyment Scale: ☺ ☺ ☺ ☺ ☺

Who Noticed: _____

Who Left The Room: _____

Date: ___ / ___ / ___   Sun Mon Tue Wed Thu Fri Sat

Time of Fart: _____ am/pm   **Duration:** ___ min ___ sec

Fart Intensity:
- ○ **Gentle Puff** (barely there, quick & unscented)
- ○ **SBD** (silent but deadly)
- ○ **Military March** (series of puffs with mild scent)
- ○ **Classic** (quick, loud, stinky scent but fades quickly)
- ○ **Thunder Rumble** (long, loud & stinky)
- ○ **Diarrhea Storm** (explosive, wet & clears the room)
- ○ **Oh, Crap!** (self explanatory)

Fart Enjoyment Scale: ☺ ☺ ☺ ☺ ☺

Who Noticed: _____

Who Left The Room: _____

NOTES

_____

_____

_____

_____

_____

_____

_____

_____

_____

_____

_____

NOTES

_____

_____

_____

_____

_____

_____

_____

_____

_____

_____

Date: ___ / ___ / ___   Sun Mon Tue Wed Thu Fri Sat

Time of Fart: _____ am/pm   **Duration:** ___ min ___ sec

Fart Intensity:
- ○ **Gentle Puff** (barely there, quick & unscented)
- ○ **SBD** (silent but deadly)
- ○ **Military March** (series of puffs with mild scent)
- ○ **Classic** (quick, loud, stinky scent but fades quickly)
- ○ **Thunder Rumble** (long, loud & stinky)
- ○ **Diarrhea Storm** (explosive, wet & clears the room)
- ○ **Oh, Crap!** (self explanatory)

Fart Enjoyment Scale: ☺ ☺ ☺ ☺ ☺

Who Noticed: _____

Who Left The Room: _____

Date: ___ / ___ / ___   Sun Mon Tue Wed Thu Fri Sat

Time of Fart: _____ am/pm   **Duration:** ___ min ___ sec

Fart Intensity:
- ○ **Gentle Puff** (barely there, quick & unscented)
- ○ **SBD** (silent but deadly)
- ○ **Military March** (series of puffs with mild scent)
- ○ **Classic** (quick, loud, stinky scent but fades quickly)
- ○ **Thunder Rumble** (long, loud & stinky)
- ○ **Diarrhea Storm** (explosive, wet & clears the room)
- ○ **Oh, Crap!** (self explanatory)

Fart Enjoyment Scale: ☺ ☺ ☺ ☺ ☺

Who Noticed: _____

Who Left The Room: _____

NOTES

NOTES

Date: ___ / ___ / ___   Sun Mon Tue Wed Thu Fri Sat

Time of Fart: _____ am/pm   **Duration:** ___ min ___ sec

Fart Intensity:
- ○ **Gentle Puff** (barely there, quick & unscented)
- ○ **SBD** (silent but deadly)
- ○ **Military March** (series of puffs with mild scent)
- ○ **Classic** (quick, loud, stinky scent but fades quickly)
- ○ **Thunder Rumble** (long, loud & stinky)
- ○ **Diarrhea Storm** (explosive, wet & clears the room)
- ○ **Oh, Crap!** (self explanatory)

Fart Enjoyment Scale: ☺ ☺ ☺ ☺ ☺

Who Noticed: _____

Who Left The Room: _____

Date: ___ / ___ / ___   Sun Mon Tue Wed Thu Fri Sat

Time of Fart: _____ am/pm   **Duration:** ___ min ___ sec

Fart Intensity:
- ○ **Gentle Puff** (barely there, quick & unscented)
- ○ **SBD** (silent but deadly)
- ○ **Military March** (series of puffs with mild scent)
- ○ **Classic** (quick, loud, stinky scent but fades quickly)
- ○ **Thunder Rumble** (long, loud & stinky)
- ○ **Diarrhea Storm** (explosive, wet & clears the room)
- ○ **Oh, Crap!** (self explanatory)

Fart Enjoyment Scale: ☺ ☺ ☺ ☺ ☺

Who Noticed: _____

Who Left The Room: _____

NOTES

_____
_____
_____
_____
_____
_____
_____
_____
_____
_____

NOTES

_____
_____
_____
_____
_____
_____
_____
_____
_____
_____

Date: ___ / ___ / ___   Sun Mon Tue Wed Thu Fri Sat

Time of Fart: _____ am/pm   **Duration:** ___ min ___ sec

Fart Intensity:
- ○ **Gentle Puff** (barely there, quick & unscented)
- ○ **SBD** (silent but deadly)
- ○ **Military March** (series of puffs with mild scent)
- ○ **Classic** (quick, loud, stinky scent but fades quickly)
- ○ **Thunder Rumble** (long, loud & stinky)
- ○ **Diarrhea Storm** (explosive, wet & clears the room)
- ○ **Oh, Crap!** (self explanatory)

Fart Enjoyment Scale: ☺ ☺ ☺ ☺ ☺

Who Noticed: _____

Who Left The Room: _____

Date: ___ / ___ / ___   Sun Mon Tue Wed Thu Fri Sat

Time of Fart: _____ am/pm   **Duration:** ___ min ___ sec

Fart Intensity:
- ○ **Gentle Puff** (barely there, quick & unscented)
- ○ **SBD** (silent but deadly)
- ○ **Military March** (series of puffs with mild scent)
- ○ **Classic** (quick, loud, stinky scent but fades quickly)
- ○ **Thunder Rumble** (long, loud & stinky)
- ○ **Diarrhea Storm** (explosive, wet & clears the room)
- ○ **Oh, Crap!** (self explanatory)

Fart Enjoyment Scale: ☺ ☺ ☺ ☺ ☺

Who Noticed: _____

Who Left The Room: _____

NOTES

_____

_____

_____

_____

_____

_____

_____

_____

_____

_____

_____

NOTES

_____

_____

_____

_____

_____

_____

_____

_____

_____

_____

Date: ___ / ___ / ___   Sun Mon Tue Wed Thu Fri Sat

Time of Fart: _____ am/pm   **Duration:** ___ min ___ sec

Fart Intensity:
- ○ **Gentle Puff** (barely there, quick & unscented)
- ○ **SBD** (silent but deadly)
- ○ **Military March** (series of puffs with mild scent)
- ○ **Classic** (quick, loud, stinky scent but fades quickly)
- ○ **Thunder Rumble** (long, loud & stinky)
- ○ **Diarrhea Storm** (explosive, wet & clears the room)
- ○ **Oh, Crap!** (self explanatory)

Fart Enjoyment Scale: ☺ ☺ ☺ ☺ ☺

Who Noticed: _____

Who Left The Room: _____

Date: ___ / ___ / ___   Sun Mon Tue Wed Thu Fri Sat

Time of Fart: _____ am/pm   **Duration:** ___ min ___ sec

Fart Intensity:
- ○ **Gentle Puff** (barely there, quick & unscented)
- ○ **SBD** (silent but deadly)
- ○ **Military March** (series of puffs with mild scent)
- ○ **Classic** (quick, loud, stinky scent but fades quickly)
- ○ **Thunder Rumble** (long, loud & stinky)
- ○ **Diarrhea Storm** (explosive, wet & clears the room)
- ○ **Oh, Crap!** (self explanatory)

Fart Enjoyment Scale: ☺ ☺ ☺ ☺ ☺

Who Noticed: _____

Who Left The Room: _____

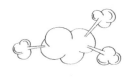 # NOTES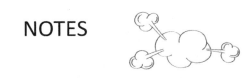

NOTES

Date: ___ / ___ / ___   Sun Mon Tue Wed Thu Fri Sat

Time of Fart: _____ am/pm   **Duration:** ___ min ___ sec

Fart Intensity:
- ○ **Gentle Puff** (barely there, quick & unscented)
- ○ **SBD** (silent but deadly)
- ○ **Military March** (series of puffs with mild scent)
- ○ **Classic** (quick, loud, stinky scent but fades quickly)
- ○ **Thunder Rumble** (long, loud & stinky)
- ○ **Diarrhea Storm** (explosive, wet & clears the room)
- ○ **Oh, Crap!** (self explanatory)

Fart Enjoyment Scale: ☺ ☺ ☺ ☺ ☺

Who Noticed: _____

Who Left The Room: _____

Date: ___ / ___ / ___   Sun Mon Tue Wed Thu Fri Sat

Time of Fart: _____ am/pm   **Duration:** ___ min ___ sec

Fart Intensity:
- ○ **Gentle Puff** (barely there, quick & unscented)
- ○ **SBD** (silent but deadly)
- ○ **Military March** (series of puffs with mild scent)
- ○ **Classic** (quick, loud, stinky scent but fades quickly)
- ○ **Thunder Rumble** (long, loud & stinky)
- ○ **Diarrhea Storm** (explosive, wet & clears the room)
- ○ **Oh, Crap!** (self explanatory)

Fart Enjoyment Scale: ☺ ☺ ☺ ☺ ☺

Who Noticed: _____

Who Left The Room: _____

NOTES

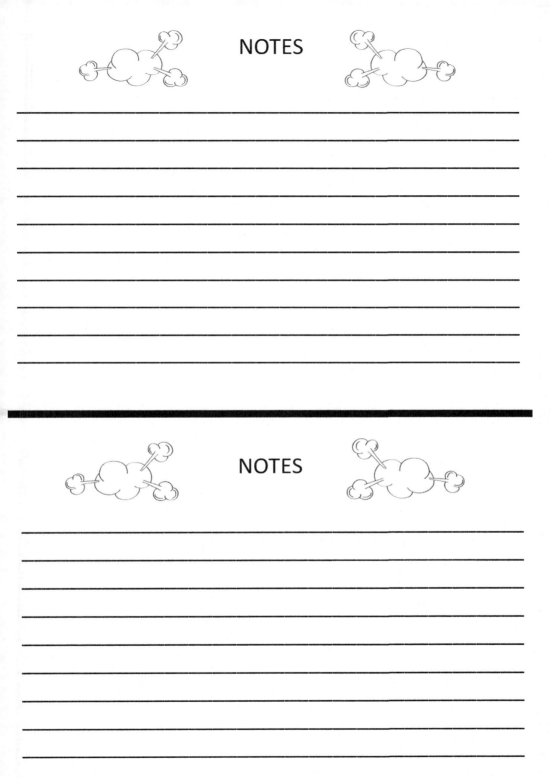

NOTES

Date: ___ / ___ / ___   Sun Mon Tue Wed Thu Fri Sat

Time of Fart: _____ am/pm   **Duration:** ___ min ___ sec

Fart Intensity:
- ○ **Gentle Puff** (barely there, quick & unscented)
- ○ **SBD** (silent but deadly)
- ○ **Military March** (series of puffs with mild scent)
- ○ **Classic** (quick, loud, stinky scent but fades quickly)
- ○ **Thunder Rumble** (long, loud & stinky)
- ○ **Diarrhea Storm** (explosive, wet & clears the room)
- ○ **Oh, Crap!** (self explanatory)

Fart Enjoyment Scale: ☺ ☺ ☺ ☺ ☺

Who Noticed: _____

Who Left The Room: _____

Date: ___ / ___ / ___   Sun Mon Tue Wed Thu Fri Sat

Time of Fart: _____ am/pm   **Duration:** ___ min ___ sec

Fart Intensity:
- ○ **Gentle Puff** (barely there, quick & unscented)
- ○ **SBD** (silent but deadly)
- ○ **Military March** (series of puffs with mild scent)
- ○ **Classic** (quick, loud, stinky scent but fades quickly)
- ○ **Thunder Rumble** (long, loud & stinky)
- ○ **Diarrhea Storm** (explosive, wet & clears the room)
- ○ **Oh, Crap!** (self explanatory)

Fart Enjoyment Scale: ☺ ☺ ☺ ☺ ☺

Who Noticed: _____

Who Left The Room: _____

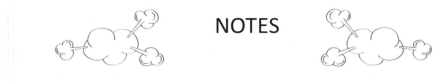

NOTES

_____

_____

_____

_____

_____

_____

_____

_____

_____

NOTES

_____

_____

_____

_____

_____

_____

_____

_____

Date: ___ / ___ / ___   Sun Mon Tue Wed Thu Fri Sat

Time of Fart: _____ am/pm   **Duration:** ___ min ___ sec

Fart Intensity:
- ○ **Gentle Puff** (barely there, quick & unscented)
- ○ **SBD** (silent but deadly)
- ○ **Military March** (series of puffs with mild scent)
- ○ **Classic** (quick, loud, stinky scent but fades quickly)
- ○ **Thunder Rumble** (long, loud & stinky)
- ○ **Diarrhea Storm** (explosive, wet & clears the room)
- ○ **Oh, Crap!** (self explanatory)

Fart Enjoyment Scale: ☺ ☺ ☺ ☺ ☺

Who Noticed: _____

Who Left The Room: _____

Date: ___ / ___ / ___   Sun Mon Tue Wed Thu Fri Sat

Time of Fart: _____ am/pm   **Duration:** ___ min ___ sec

Fart Intensity:
- ○ **Gentle Puff** (barely there, quick & unscented)
- ○ **SBD** (silent but deadly)
- ○ **Military March** (series of puffs with mild scent)
- ○ **Classic** (quick, loud, stinky scent but fades quickly)
- ○ **Thunder Rumble** (long, loud & stinky)
- ○ **Diarrhea Storm** (explosive, wet & clears the room)
- ○ **Oh, Crap!** (self explanatory)

Fart Enjoyment Scale: ☺ ☺ ☺ ☺ ☺

Who Noticed: _____

Who Left The Room: _____

NOTES

NOTES

Date: ___ / ___ / ___   Sun Mon Tue Wed Thu Fri Sat

Time of Fart: _____ am/pm   **Duration:** ___ min ___ sec

Fart Intensity:

- ○ **Gentle Puff** (barely there, quick & unscented)
- ○ **SBD** (silent but deadly)
- ○ **Military March** (series of puffs with mild scent)
- ○ **Classic** (quick, loud, stinky scent but fades quickly)
- ○ **Thunder Rumble** (long, loud & stinky)
- ○ **Diarrhea Storm** (explosive, wet & clears the room)
- ○ **Oh, Crap!** (self explanatory)

Fart Enjoyment Scale: ☺ ☺ ☺ ☺ ☺

Who Noticed: _____

Who Left The Room: _____

Date: ___ / ___ / ___   Sun Mon Tue Wed Thu Fri Sat

Time of Fart: _____ am/pm   **Duration:** ___ min ___ sec

Fart Intensity:

- ○ **Gentle Puff** (barely there, quick & unscented)
- ○ **SBD** (silent but deadly)
- ○ **Military March** (series of puffs with mild scent)
- ○ **Classic** (quick, loud, stinky scent but fades quickly)
- ○ **Thunder Rumble** (long, loud & stinky)
- ○ **Diarrhea Storm** (explosive, wet & clears the room)
- ○ **Oh, Crap!** (self explanatory)

Fart Enjoyment Scale: ☺ ☺ ☺ ☺ ☺

Who Noticed: _____

Who Left The Room: _____

NOTES

NOTES

Date: ___ / ___ / ___   Sun   Mon   Tue   Wed   Thu   Fri   Sat

Time of Fart: _____ am/pm   **Duration:** ___ min ___ sec

Fart Intensity:
- ○ **Gentle Puff** (barely there, quick & unscented)
- ○ **SBD** (silent but deadly)
- ○ **Military March** (series of puffs with mild scent)
- ○ **Classic** (quick, loud, stinky scent but fades quickly)
- ○ **Thunder Rumble** (long, loud & stinky)
- ○ **Diarrhea Storm** (explosive, wet & clears the room)
- ○ **Oh, Crap!** (self explanatory)

Fart Enjoyment Scale: ☺ ☺ ☺ ☺ ☺

Who Noticed: _____

Who Left The Room: _____

Date: ___ / ___ / ___   Sun   Mon   Tue   Wed   Thu   Fri   Sat

Time of Fart: _____ am/pm   **Duration:** ___ min ___ sec

Fart Intensity:
- ○ **Gentle Puff** (barely there, quick & unscented)
- ○ **SBD** (silent but deadly)
- ○ **Military March** (series of puffs with mild scent)
- ○ **Classic** (quick, loud, stinky scent but fades quickly)
- ○ **Thunder Rumble** (long, loud & stinky)
- ○ **Diarrhea Storm** (explosive, wet & clears the room)
- ○ **Oh, Crap!** (self explanatory)

Fart Enjoyment Scale: ☺ ☺ ☺ ☺ ☺

Who Noticed: _____

Who Left The Room: _____

NOTES

NOTES

Date: ___ / ___ / ___   Sun Mon Tue Wed Thu Fri Sat

Time of Fart: _____ am/pm   **Duration:** ___ min ___ sec

Fart Intensity:
- ○ **Gentle Puff** (barely there, quick & unscented)
- ○ **SBD** (silent but deadly)
- ○ **Military March** (series of puffs with mild scent)
- ○ **Classic** (quick, loud, stinky scent but fades quickly)
- ○ **Thunder Rumble** (long, loud & stinky)
- ○ **Diarrhea Storm** (explosive, wet & clears the room)
- ○ **Oh, Crap!** (self explanatory)

Fart Enjoyment Scale: ☺ ☺ ☺ ☺ ☺

Who Noticed: _____

Who Left The Room: _____

Date: ___ / ___ / ___   Sun Mon Tue Wed Thu Fri Sat

Time of Fart: _____ am/pm   **Duration:** ___ min ___ sec

Fart Intensity:
- ○ **Gentle Puff** (barely there, quick & unscented)
- ○ **SBD** (silent but deadly)
- ○ **Military March** (series of puffs with mild scent)
- ○ **Classic** (quick, loud, stinky scent but fades quickly)
- ○ **Thunder Rumble** (long, loud & stinky)
- ○ **Diarrhea Storm** (explosive, wet & clears the room)
- ○ **Oh, Crap!** (self explanatory)

Fart Enjoyment Scale: ☺ ☺ ☺ ☺ ☺

Who Noticed: _____

Who Left The Room: _____

NOTES

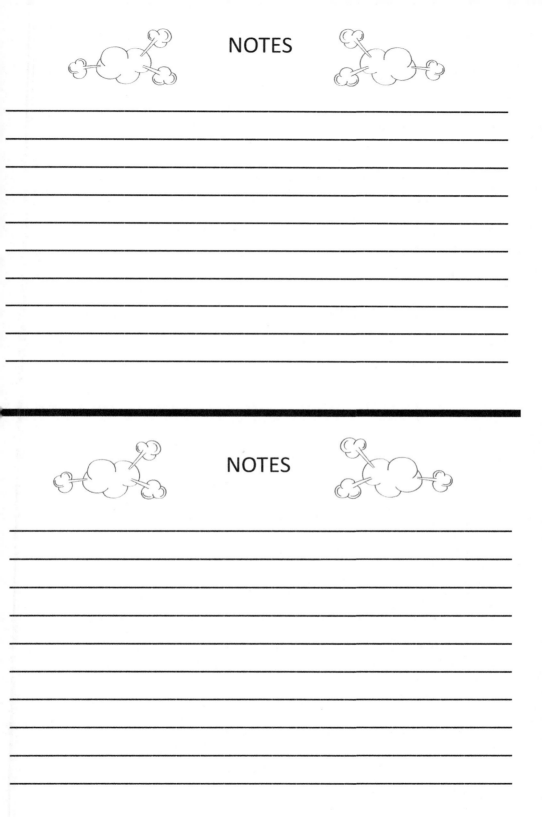

NOTES

Date: ___ / ___ / ___   Sun Mon Tue Wed Thu Fri Sat

Time of Fart: _____ am/pm   **Duration:** ___ min ___ sec

Fart Intensity:
- ○ **Gentle Puff** (barely there, quick & unscented)
- ○ **SBD** (silent but deadly)
- ○ **Military March** (series of puffs with mild scent)
- ○ **Classic** (quick, loud, stinky scent but fades quickly)
- ○ **Thunder Rumble** (long, loud & stinky)
- ○ **Diarrhea Storm** (explosive, wet & clears the room)
- ○ **Oh, Crap!** (self explanatory)

Fart Enjoyment Scale: ☺ ☺ ☺ ☺ ☺

Who Noticed: _____

Who Left The Room: _____

Date: ___ / ___ / ___   Sun Mon Tue Wed Thu Fri Sat

Time of Fart: _____ am/pm   **Duration:** ___ min ___ sec

Fart Intensity:
- ○ **Gentle Puff** (barely there, quick & unscented)
- ○ **SBD** (silent but deadly)
- ○ **Military March** (series of puffs with mild scent)
- ○ **Classic** (quick, loud, stinky scent but fades quickly)
- ○ **Thunder Rumble** (long, loud & stinky)
- ○ **Diarrhea Storm** (explosive, wet & clears the room)
- ○ **Oh, Crap!** (self explanatory)

Fart Enjoyment Scale: ☺ ☺ ☺ ☺ ☺

Who Noticed: _____

Who Left The Room: _____

NOTES

_____
_____
_____
_____
_____
_____
_____
_____
_____
_____
_____

NOTES

_____
_____
_____
_____
_____
_____
_____
_____
_____
_____

Date: ___ / ___ / ___   Sun   Mon   Tue   Wed   Thu   Fri   Sat

Time of Fart: _____ am/pm   **Duration:** ___ min ___ sec

Fart Intensity:
- ○ **Gentle Puff** (barely there, quick & unscented)
- ○ **SBD** (silent but deadly)
- ○ **Military March** (series of puffs with mild scent)
- ○ **Classic** (quick, loud, stinky scent but fades quickly)
- ○ **Thunder Rumble** (long, loud & stinky)
- ○ **Diarrhea Storm** (explosive, wet & clears the room)
- ○ **Oh, Crap!** (self explanatory)

Fart Enjoyment Scale: ☺ ☺ ☺ ☺ ☺

Who Noticed: _____

Who Left The Room: _____

Date: ___ / ___ / ___   Sun   Mon   Tue   Wed   Thu   Fri   Sat

Time of Fart: _____ am/pm   **Duration:** ___ min ___ sec

Fart Intensity:
- ○ **Gentle Puff** (barely there, quick & unscented)
- ○ **SBD** (silent but deadly)
- ○ **Military March** (series of puffs with mild scent)
- ○ **Classic** (quick, loud, stinky scent but fades quickly)
- ○ **Thunder Rumble** (long, loud & stinky)
- ○ **Diarrhea Storm** (explosive, wet & clears the room)
- ○ **Oh, Crap!** (self explanatory)

Fart Enjoyment Scale: ☺ ☺ ☺ ☺ ☺

Who Noticed: _____

Who Left The Room: _____

NOTES

_____
_____
_____
_____
_____
_____
_____
_____
_____
_____

NOTES

_____
_____
_____
_____
_____
_____
_____
_____
_____
_____

Date: ___ / ___ / ___   Sun Mon Tue Wed Thu Fri Sat

Time of Fart: _____ am/pm   **Duration:** ___ min ___ sec

Fart Intensity:
- ○ **Gentle Puff** (barely there, quick & unscented)
- ○ **SBD** (silent but deadly)
- ○ **Military March** (series of puffs with mild scent)
- ○ **Classic** (quick, loud, stinky scent but fades quickly)
- ○ **Thunder Rumble** (long, loud & stinky)
- ○ **Diarrhea Storm** (explosive, wet & clears the room)
- ○ **Oh, Crap!** (self explanatory)

Fart Enjoyment Scale: ☺ ☺ ☺ ☺ ☺

Who Noticed: _____

Who Left The Room: _____

Date: ___ / ___ / ___   Sun Mon Tue Wed Thu Fri Sat

Time of Fart: _____ am/pm   **Duration:** ___ min ___ sec

Fart Intensity:
- ○ **Gentle Puff** (barely there, quick & unscented)
- ○ **SBD** (silent but deadly)
- ○ **Military March** (series of puffs with mild scent)
- ○ **Classic** (quick, loud, stinky scent but fades quickly)
- ○ **Thunder Rumble** (long, loud & stinky)
- ○ **Diarrhea Storm** (explosive, wet & clears the room)
- ○ **Oh, Crap!** (self explanatory)

Fart Enjoyment Scale: ☺ ☺ ☺ ☺ ☺

Who Noticed: _____

Who Left The Room: _____

NOTES

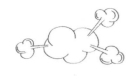 

_____
_____
_____
_____
_____
_____
_____
_____
_____
_____
_____

NOTES

_____
_____
_____
_____
_____
_____
_____
_____
_____
_____

Date: ___ / ___ / ___   Sun   Mon   Tue   Wed   Thu   Fri   Sat

Time of Fart: _____ am/pm   **Duration:** ___ min ___ sec

Fart Intensity:
- ○ **Gentle Puff** (barely there, quick & unscented)
- ○ **SBD** (silent but deadly)
- ○ **Military March** (series of puffs with mild scent)
- ○ **Classic** (quick, loud, stinky scent but fades quickly)
- ○ **Thunder Rumble** (long, loud & stinky)
- ○ **Diarrhea Storm** (explosive, wet & clears the room)
- ○ **Oh, Crap!** (self explanatory)

Fart Enjoyment Scale: ☺ ☺ ☺ ☺ ☺

Who Noticed: _____

Who Left The Room: _____

Date: ___ / ___ / ___   Sun   Mon   Tue   Wed   Thu   Fri   Sat

Time of Fart: _____ am/pm   **Duration:** ___ min ___ sec

Fart Intensity:
- ○ **Gentle Puff** (barely there, quick & unscented)
- ○ **SBD** (silent but deadly)
- ○ **Military March** (series of puffs with mild scent)
- ○ **Classic** (quick, loud, stinky scent but fades quickly)
- ○ **Thunder Rumble** (long, loud & stinky)
- ○ **Diarrhea Storm** (explosive, wet & clears the room)
- ○ **Oh, Crap!** (self explanatory)

Fart Enjoyment Scale: ☺ ☺ ☺ ☺ ☺

Who Noticed: _____

Who Left The Room: _____

NOTES

NOTES

Date: ___ / ___ / ___   Sun Mon Tue Wed Thu Fri Sat

Time of Fart: _____ am/pm   **Duration:** ___ min ___ sec

Fart Intensity:
- ○ **Gentle Puff** (barely there, quick & unscented)
- ○ **SBD** (silent but deadly)
- ○ **Military March** (series of puffs with mild scent)
- ○ **Classic** (quick, loud, stinky scent but fades quickly)
- ○ **Thunder Rumble** (long, loud & stinky)
- ○ **Diarrhea Storm** (explosive, wet & clears the room)
- ○ **Oh, Crap!** (self explanatory)

Fart Enjoyment Scale: ☺ ☺ ☺ ☺ ☺

Who Noticed: _____

Who Left The Room: _____

Date: ___ / ___ / ___   Sun Mon Tue Wed Thu Fri Sat

Time of Fart: _____ am/pm   **Duration:** ___ min ___ sec

Fart Intensity:
- ○ **Gentle Puff** (barely there, quick & unscented)
- ○ **SBD** (silent but deadly)
- ○ **Military March** (series of puffs with mild scent)
- ○ **Classic** (quick, loud, stinky scent but fades quickly)
- ○ **Thunder Rumble** (long, loud & stinky)
- ○ **Diarrhea Storm** (explosive, wet & clears the room)
- ○ **Oh, Crap!** (self explanatory)

Fart Enjoyment Scale: ☺ ☺ ☺ ☺ ☺

Who Noticed: _____

Who Left The Room: _____

NOTES

_____

_____

_____

_____

_____

_____

_____

_____

_____

_____

NOTES

_____

_____

_____

_____

_____

_____

_____

_____

_____

_____

Date: ___ / ___ / ___   Sun Mon Tue Wed Thu Fri Sat

Time of Fart: _____ am/pm   **Duration:** ___ min ___ sec

Fart Intensity:
- ○ **Gentle Puff** (barely there, quick & unscented)
- ○ **SBD** (silent but deadly)
- ○ **Military March** (series of puffs with mild scent)
- ○ **Classic** (quick, loud, stinky scent but fades quickly)
- ○ **Thunder Rumble** (long, loud & stinky)
- ○ **Diarrhea Storm** (explosive, wet & clears the room)
- ○ **Oh, Crap!** (self explanatory)

Fart Enjoyment Scale: ☺ ☺ ☺ ☺ ☺

Who Noticed: _____

Who Left The Room: _____

Date: ___ / ___ / ___   Sun Mon Tue Wed Thu Fri Sat

Time of Fart: _____ am/pm   **Duration:** ___ min ___ sec

Fart Intensity:
- ○ **Gentle Puff** (barely there, quick & unscented)
- ○ **SBD** (silent but deadly)
- ○ **Military March** (series of puffs with mild scent)
- ○ **Classic** (quick, loud, stinky scent but fades quickly)
- ○ **Thunder Rumble** (long, loud & stinky)
- ○ **Diarrhea Storm** (explosive, wet & clears the room)
- ○ **Oh, Crap!** (self explanatory)

Fart Enjoyment Scale: ☺ ☺ ☺ ☺ ☺

Who Noticed: _____

Who Left The Room: _____

NOTES

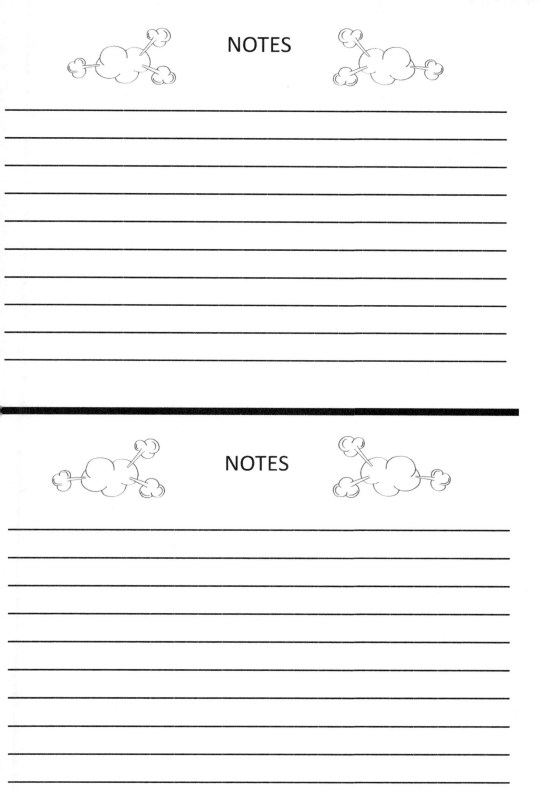

NOTES

Date: ___ / ___ / ___   Sun Mon Tue Wed Thu Fri Sat

Time of Fart: _____ am/pm   **Duration:** ___ min ___ sec

Fart Intensity:
- ○ **Gentle Puff** (barely there, quick & unscented)
- ○ **SBD** (silent but deadly)
- ○ **Military March** (series of puffs with mild scent)
- ○ **Classic** (quick, loud, stinky scent but fades quickly)
- ○ **Thunder Rumble** (long, loud & stinky)
- ○ **Diarrhea Storm** (explosive, wet & clears the room)
- ○ **Oh, Crap!** (self explanatory)

Fart Enjoyment Scale: ☺ ☺ ☺ ☺ ☺

Who Noticed: _____

Who Left The Room: _____

Date: ___ / ___ / ___   Sun Mon Tue Wed Thu Fri Sat

Time of Fart: _____ am/pm   **Duration:** ___ min ___ sec

Fart Intensity:
- ○ **Gentle Puff** (barely there, quick & unscented)
- ○ **SBD** (silent but deadly)
- ○ **Military March** (series of puffs with mild scent)
- ○ **Classic** (quick, loud, stinky scent but fades quickly)
- ○ **Thunder Rumble** (long, loud & stinky)
- ○ **Diarrhea Storm** (explosive, wet & clears the room)
- ○ **Oh, Crap!** (self explanatory)

Fart Enjoyment Scale: ☺ ☺ ☺ ☺ ☺

Who Noticed: _____

Who Left The Room: _____

NOTES

_____
_____
_____
_____
_____
_____
_____
_____
_____
_____

NOTES

_____
_____
_____
_____
_____
_____
_____
_____
_____

Date: ___ / ___ / ___   Sun Mon Tue Wed Thu Fri Sat

Time of Fart: _____ am/pm   **Duration:** ___ min ___ sec

Fart Intensity:
- ○ **Gentle Puff** (barely there, quick & unscented)
- ○ **SBD** (silent but deadly)
- ○ **Military March** (series of puffs with mild scent)
- ○ **Classic** (quick, loud, stinky scent but fades quickly)
- ○ **Thunder Rumble** (long, loud & stinky)
- ○ **Diarrhea Storm** (explosive, wet & clears the room)
- ○ **Oh, Crap!** (self explanatory)

Fart Enjoyment Scale: ☺ ☺ ☺ ☺ ☺

Who Noticed: _____

Who Left The Room: _____

Date: ___ / ___ / ___   Sun Mon Tue Wed Thu Fri Sat

Time of Fart: _____ am/pm   **Duration:** ___ min ___ sec

Fart Intensity:
- ○ **Gentle Puff** (barely there, quick & unscented)
- ○ **SBD** (silent but deadly)
- ○ **Military March** (series of puffs with mild scent)
- ○ **Classic** (quick, loud, stinky scent but fades quickly)
- ○ **Thunder Rumble** (long, loud & stinky)
- ○ **Diarrhea Storm** (explosive, wet & clears the room)
- ○ **Oh, Crap!** (self explanatory)

Fart Enjoyment Scale: ☺ ☺ ☺ ☺ ☺

Who Noticed: _____

Who Left The Room: _____

NOTES

NOTES

Date: ___ / ___ / ___   Sun Mon Tue Wed Thu Fri Sat

Time of Fart: _____ am/pm   **Duration:** ___ min ___ sec

Fart Intensity:
- ○ **Gentle Puff** (barely there, quick & unscented)
- ○ **SBD** (silent but deadly)
- ○ **Military March** (series of puffs with mild scent)
- ○ **Classic** (quick, loud, stinky scent but fades quickly)
- ○ **Thunder Rumble** (long, loud & stinky)
- ○ **Diarrhea Storm** (explosive, wet & clears the room)
- ○ **Oh, Crap!** (self explanatory)

Fart Enjoyment Scale: ☺ ☺ ☺ ☺ ☺

Who Noticed: _____

Who Left The Room: _____

Date: ___ / ___ / ___   Sun Mon Tue Wed Thu Fri Sat

Time of Fart: _____ am/pm   **Duration:** ___ min ___ sec

Fart Intensity:
- ○ **Gentle Puff** (barely there, quick & unscented)
- ○ **SBD** (silent but deadly)
- ○ **Military March** (series of puffs with mild scent)
- ○ **Classic** (quick, loud, stinky scent but fades quickly)
- ○ **Thunder Rumble** (long, loud & stinky)
- ○ **Diarrhea Storm** (explosive, wet & clears the room)
- ○ **Oh, Crap!** (self explanatory)

Fart Enjoyment Scale: ☺ ☺ ☺ ☺ ☺

Who Noticed: _____

Who Left The Room: _____

NOTES

NOTES

Date: ___ / ___ / ___   Sun Mon Tue Wed Thu Fri Sat

Time of Fart: _____ am/pm   **Duration:** ___ min ___ sec

Fart Intensity:

- ○ **Gentle Puff** (barely there, quick & unscented)
- ○ **SBD** (silent but deadly)
- ○ **Military March** (series of puffs with mild scent)
- ○ **Classic** (quick, loud, stinky scent but fades quickly)
- ○ **Thunder Rumble** (long, loud & stinky)
- ○ **Diarrhea Storm** (explosive, wet & clears the room)
- ○ **Oh, Crap!** (self explanatory)

Fart Enjoyment Scale: ☺ ☺ ☺ ☺ ☺

Who Noticed: _____

Who Left The Room: _____

Date: ___ / ___ / ___   Sun Mon Tue Wed Thu Fri Sat

Time of Fart: _____ am/pm   **Duration:** ___ min ___ sec

Fart Intensity:

- ○ **Gentle Puff** (barely there, quick & unscented)
- ○ **SBD** (silent but deadly)
- ○ **Military March** (series of puffs with mild scent)
- ○ **Classic** (quick, loud, stinky scent but fades quickly)
- ○ **Thunder Rumble** (long, loud & stinky)
- ○ **Diarrhea Storm** (explosive, wet & clears the room)
- ○ **Oh, Crap!** (self explanatory)

Fart Enjoyment Scale: ☺ ☺ ☺ ☺ ☺

Who Noticed: _____

Who Left The Room: _____

NOTES

NOTES

Date: ___ / ___ / ___   Sun   Mon   Tue   Wed   Thu   Fri   Sat

Time of Fart: _____ am/pm   **Duration:** ___ min ___ sec

Fart Intensity:
- ○ **Gentle Puff** (barely there, quick & unscented)
- ○ **SBD** (silent but deadly)
- ○ **Military March** (series of puffs with mild scent)
- ○ **Classic** (quick, loud, stinky scent but fades quickly)
- ○ **Thunder Rumble** (long, loud & stinky)
- ○ **Diarrhea Storm** (explosive, wet & clears the room)
- ○ **Oh, Crap!** (self explanatory)

Fart Enjoyment Scale: 😊 😊 😊 😊 😊

Who Noticed: _____

Who Left The Room: _____

Date: ___ / ___ / ___   Sun   Mon   Tue   Wed   Thu   Fri   Sat

Time of Fart: _____ am/pm   **Duration:** ___ min ___ sec

Fart Intensity:
- ○ **Gentle Puff** (barely there, quick & unscented)
- ○ **SBD** (silent but deadly)
- ○ **Military March** (series of puffs with mild scent)
- ○ **Classic** (quick, loud, stinky scent but fades quickly)
- ○ **Thunder Rumble** (long, loud & stinky)
- ○ **Diarrhea Storm** (explosive, wet & clears the room)
- ○ **Oh, Crap!** (self explanatory)

Fart Enjoyment Scale: 😊 😊 😊 😊 😊

Who Noticed: _____

Who Left The Room: _____

NOTES

NOTES

Date: ___ / ___ / ___   Sun Mon Tue Wed Thu Fri Sat

Time of Fart: _____ am/pm   **Duration:** ___ min ___ sec

Fart Intensity:
- ○ **Gentle Puff** (barely there, quick & unscented)
- ○ **SBD** (silent but deadly)
- ○ **Military March** (series of puffs with mild scent)
- ○ **Classic** (quick, loud, stinky scent but fades quickly)
- ○ **Thunder Rumble** (long, loud & stinky)
- ○ **Diarrhea Storm** (explosive, wet & clears the room)
- ○ **Oh, Crap!** (self explanatory)

Fart Enjoyment Scale: ☺ ☺ ☺ ☺ ☺

Who Noticed: _____

Who Left The Room: _____

Date: ___ / ___ / ___   Sun Mon Tue Wed Thu Fri Sat

Time of Fart: _____ am/pm   **Duration:** ___ min ___ sec

Fart Intensity:
- ○ **Gentle Puff** (barely there, quick & unscented)
- ○ **SBD** (silent but deadly)
- ○ **Military March** (series of puffs with mild scent)
- ○ **Classic** (quick, loud, stinky scent but fades quickly)
- ○ **Thunder Rumble** (long, loud & stinky)
- ○ **Diarrhea Storm** (explosive, wet & clears the room)
- ○ **Oh, Crap!** (self explanatory)

Fart Enjoyment Scale: ☺ ☺ ☺ ☺ ☺

Who Noticed: _____

Who Left The Room: _____

# NOTES

NOTES

Date: ___ / ___ / ___   Sun Mon Tue Wed Thu Fri Sat

Time of Fart: _____ am/pm   **Duration:** ___ min ___ sec

Fart Intensity:
- ○ **Gentle Puff** (barely there, quick & unscented)
- ○ **SBD** (silent but deadly)
- ○ **Military March** (series of puffs with mild scent)
- ○ **Classic** (quick, loud, stinky scent but fades quickly)
- ○ **Thunder Rumble** (long, loud & stinky)
- ○ **Diarrhea Storm** (explosive, wet & clears the room)
- ○ **Oh, Crap!** (self explanatory)

Fart Enjoyment Scale: ☺ ☺ ☺ ☺ ☺

Who Noticed: _____

Who Left The Room: _____

Date: ___ / ___ / ___   Sun Mon Tue Wed Thu Fri Sat

Time of Fart: _____ am/pm   **Duration:** ___ min ___ sec

Fart Intensity:
- ○ **Gentle Puff** (barely there, quick & unscented)
- ○ **SBD** (silent but deadly)
- ○ **Military March** (series of puffs with mild scent)
- ○ **Classic** (quick, loud, stinky scent but fades quickly)
- ○ **Thunder Rumble** (long, loud & stinky)
- ○ **Diarrhea Storm** (explosive, wet & clears the room)
- ○ **Oh, Crap!** (self explanatory)

Fart Enjoyment Scale: ☺ ☺ ☺ ☺ ☺

Who Noticed: _____

Who Left The Room: _____

NOTES

_____
_____
_____
_____
_____
_____
_____
_____
_____
_____
_____

NOTES

_____
_____
_____
_____
_____
_____
_____
_____
_____
_____
_____

Date: ___ / ___ / ___   Sun Mon Tue Wed Thu Fri Sat

Time of Fart: _____ am/pm   **Duration:** ___ min ___ sec

Fart Intensity:
- ○ **Gentle Puff** (barely there, quick & unscented)
- ○ **SBD** (silent but deadly)
- ○ **Military March** (series of puffs with mild scent)
- ○ **Classic** (quick, loud, stinky scent but fades quickly)
- ○ **Thunder Rumble** (long, loud & stinky)
- ○ **Diarrhea Storm** (explosive, wet & clears the room)
- ○ **Oh, Crap!** (self explanatory)

Fart Enjoyment Scale: ☺ ☺ ☺ ☺ ☺

Who Noticed: _____

Who Left The Room: _____

Date: ___ / ___ / ___   Sun Mon Tue Wed Thu Fri Sat

Time of Fart: _____ am/pm   **Duration:** ___ min ___ sec

Fart Intensity:
- ○ **Gentle Puff** (barely there, quick & unscented)
- ○ **SBD** (silent but deadly)
- ○ **Military March** (series of puffs with mild scent)
- ○ **Classic** (quick, loud, stinky scent but fades quickly)
- ○ **Thunder Rumble** (long, loud & stinky)
- ○ **Diarrhea Storm** (explosive, wet & clears the room)
- ○ **Oh, Crap!** (self explanatory)

Fart Enjoyment Scale: ☺ ☺ ☺ ☺ ☺

Who Noticed: _____

Who Left The Room: _____

NOTES

NOTES

Date: ___ / ___ / ___   Sun Mon Tue Wed Thu Fri Sat

Time of Fart: _____ am/pm   **Duration:** ___ min ___ sec

Fart Intensity:
- ○ **Gentle Puff** (barely there, quick & unscented)
- ○ **SBD** (silent but deadly)
- ○ **Military March** (series of puffs with mild scent)
- ○ **Classic** (quick, loud, stinky scent but fades quickly)
- ○ **Thunder Rumble** (long, loud & stinky)
- ○ **Diarrhea Storm** (explosive, wet & clears the room)
- ○ **Oh, Crap!** (self explanatory)

Fart Enjoyment Scale: ☺ ☺ ☺ ☺ ☺

Who Noticed: _____

Who Left The Room: _____

Date: ___ / ___ / ___   Sun Mon Tue Wed Thu Fri Sat

Time of Fart: _____ am/pm   **Duration:** ___ min ___ sec

Fart Intensity:
- ○ **Gentle Puff** (barely there, quick & unscented)
- ○ **SBD** (silent but deadly)
- ○ **Military March** (series of puffs with mild scent)
- ○ **Classic** (quick, loud, stinky scent but fades quickly)
- ○ **Thunder Rumble** (long, loud & stinky)
- ○ **Diarrhea Storm** (explosive, wet & clears the room)
- ○ **Oh, Crap!** (self explanatory)

Fart Enjoyment Scale: ☺ ☺ ☺ ☺ ☺

Who Noticed: _____

Who Left The Room: _____

NOTES

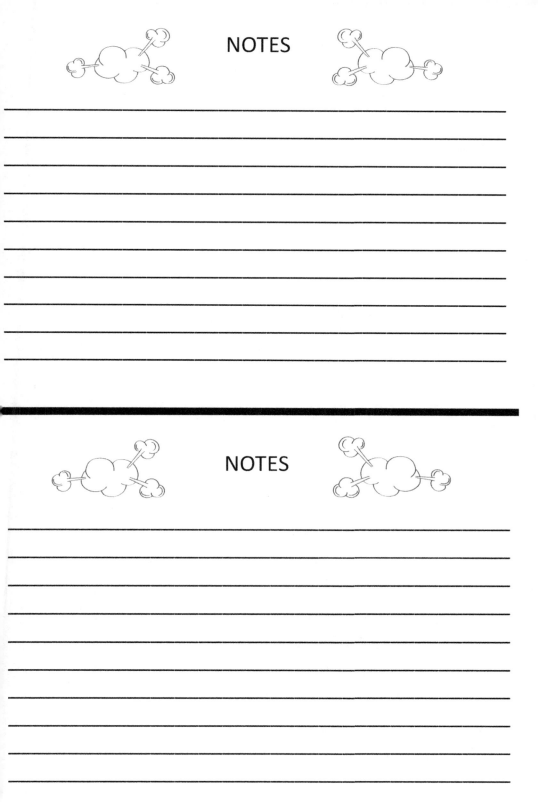

NOTES

Date: ___ / ___ / ___   Sun Mon Tue Wed Thu Fri Sat

Time of Fart: _____ am/pm   **Duration:** ___ min ___ sec

Fart Intensity:
- ○ **Gentle Puff** (barely there, quick & unscented)
- ○ **SBD** (silent but deadly)
- ○ **Military March** (series of puffs with mild scent)
- ○ **Classic** (quick, loud, stinky scent but fades quickly)
- ○ **Thunder Rumble** (long, loud & stinky)
- ○ **Diarrhea Storm** (explosive, wet & clears the room)
- ○ **Oh, Crap!** (self explanatory)

Fart Enjoyment Scale: ☺ ☺ ☺ ☺ ☺

Who Noticed: _____

Who Left The Room: _____

Date: ___ / ___ / ___   Sun Mon Tue Wed Thu Fri Sat

Time of Fart: _____ am/pm   **Duration:** ___ min ___ sec

Fart Intensity:
- ○ **Gentle Puff** (barely there, quick & unscented)
- ○ **SBD** (silent but deadly)
- ○ **Military March** (series of puffs with mild scent)
- ○ **Classic** (quick, loud, stinky scent but fades quickly)
- ○ **Thunder Rumble** (long, loud & stinky)
- ○ **Diarrhea Storm** (explosive, wet & clears the room)
- ○ **Oh, Crap!** (self explanatory)

Fart Enjoyment Scale: ☺ ☺ ☺ ☺ ☺

Who Noticed: _____

Who Left The Room: _____

 # NOTES

 # NOTES

Date: ___ / ___ / ___   Sun   Mon   Tue   Wed   Thu   Fri   Sat

Time of Fart: _____ am/pm   **Duration:** ___ min ___ sec

Fart Intensity:

- ○ **Gentle Puff** (barely there, quick & unscented)
- ○ **SBD** (silent but deadly)
- ○ **Military March** (series of puffs with mild scent)
- ○ **Classic** (quick, loud, stinky scent but fades quickly)
- ○ **Thunder Rumble** (long, loud & stinky)
- ○ **Diarrhea Storm** (explosive, wet & clears the room)
- ○ **Oh, Crap!** (self explanatory)

Fart Enjoyment Scale: ☺ ☺ ☺ ☺ ☺

Who Noticed: _____

Who Left The Room: _____

Date: ___ / ___ / ___   Sun   Mon   Tue   Wed   Thu   Fri   Sat

Time of Fart: _____ am/pm   **Duration:** ___ min ___ sec

Fart Intensity:

- ○ **Gentle Puff** (barely there, quick & unscented)
- ○ **SBD** (silent but deadly)
- ○ **Military March** (series of puffs with mild scent)
- ○ **Classic** (quick, loud, stinky scent but fades quickly)
- ○ **Thunder Rumble** (long, loud & stinky)
- ○ **Diarrhea Storm** (explosive, wet & clears the room)
- ○ **Oh, Crap!** (self explanatory)

Fart Enjoyment Scale: ☺ ☺ ☺ ☺ ☺

Who Noticed: _____

Who Left The Room: _____

NOTES

NOTES

Date: ___ / ___ / ___   Sun Mon Tue Wed Thu Fri Sat

Time of Fart: _____ am/pm   **Duration:** ___ min ___ sec

Fart Intensity:
- ○ **Gentle Puff** (barely there, quick & unscented)
- ○ **SBD** (silent but deadly)
- ○ **Military March** (series of puffs with mild scent)
- ○ **Classic** (quick, loud, stinky scent but fades quickly)
- ○ **Thunder Rumble** (long, loud & stinky)
- ○ **Diarrhea Storm** (explosive, wet & clears the room)
- ○ **Oh, Crap!** (self explanatory)

Fart Enjoyment Scale: ☺ ☺ ☺ ☺ ☺

Who Noticed: _____

Who Left The Room: _____

Date: ___ / ___ / ___   Sun Mon Tue Wed Thu Fri Sat

Time of Fart: _____ am/pm   **Duration:** ___ min ___ sec

Fart Intensity:
- ○ **Gentle Puff** (barely there, quick & unscented)
- ○ **SBD** (silent but deadly)
- ○ **Military March** (series of puffs with mild scent)
- ○ **Classic** (quick, loud, stinky scent but fades quickly)
- ○ **Thunder Rumble** (long, loud & stinky)
- ○ **Diarrhea Storm** (explosive, wet & clears the room)
- ○ **Oh, Crap!** (self explanatory)

Fart Enjoyment Scale: ☺ ☺ ☺ ☺ ☺

Who Noticed: _____

Who Left The Room: _____

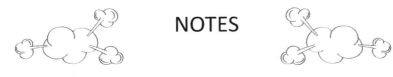

NOTES

_____
_____
_____
_____
_____
_____
_____
_____
_____
_____

NOTES

_____
_____
_____
_____
_____
_____
_____
_____
_____
_____
_____
_____
_____

Date: ___ / ___ / ___   Sun Mon Tue Wed Thu Fri Sat

Time of Fart: _____ am/pm   **Duration:** ___ min ___ sec

Fart Intensity:

- ○ **Gentle Puff** (barely there, quick & unscented)
- ○ **SBD** (silent but deadly)
- ○ **Military March** (series of puffs with mild scent)
- ○ **Classic** (quick, loud, stinky scent but fades quickly)
- ○ **Thunder Rumble** (long, loud & stinky)
- ○ **Diarrhea Storm** (explosive, wet & clears the room)
- ○ **Oh, Crap!** (self explanatory)

Fart Enjoyment Scale: ☺ ☺ ☺ ☺ ☺

Who Noticed: _____

Who Left The Room: _____

Date: ___ / ___ / ___   Sun Mon Tue Wed Thu Fri Sat

Time of Fart: _____ am/pm   **Duration:** ___ min ___ sec

Fart Intensity:

- ○ **Gentle Puff** (barely there, quick & unscented)
- ○ **SBD** (silent but deadly)
- ○ **Military March** (series of puffs with mild scent)
- ○ **Classic** (quick, loud, stinky scent but fades quickly)
- ○ **Thunder Rumble** (long, loud & stinky)
- ○ **Diarrhea Storm** (explosive, wet & clears the room)
- ○ **Oh, Crap!** (self explanatory)

Fart Enjoyment Scale: ☺ ☺ ☺ ☺ ☺

Who Noticed: _____

Who Left The Room: _____

NOTES

NOTES

Date: ___ / ___ / ___   Sun Mon Tue Wed Thu Fri Sat

Time of Fart: _____ am/pm   **Duration:** ___ min ___ sec

Fart Intensity:
- ○ **Gentle Puff** (barely there, quick & unscented)
- ○ **SBD** (silent but deadly)
- ○ **Military March** (series of puffs with mild scent)
- ○ **Classic** (quick, loud, stinky scent but fades quickly)
- ○ **Thunder Rumble** (long, loud & stinky)
- ○ **Diarrhea Storm** (explosive, wet & clears the room)
- ○ **Oh, Crap!** (self explanatory)

Fart Enjoyment Scale: ☺ ☺ ☺ ☺ ☺

Who Noticed: _____

Who Left The Room: _____

Date: ___ / ___ / ___   Sun Mon Tue Wed Thu Fri Sat

Time of Fart: _____ am/pm   **Duration:** ___ min ___ sec

Fart Intensity:
- ○ **Gentle Puff** (barely there, quick & unscented)
- ○ **SBD** (silent but deadly)
- ○ **Military March** (series of puffs with mild scent)
- ○ **Classic** (quick, loud, stinky scent but fades quickly)
- ○ **Thunder Rumble** (long, loud & stinky)
- ○ **Diarrhea Storm** (explosive, wet & clears the room)
- ○ **Oh, Crap!** (self explanatory)

Fart Enjoyment Scale: ☺ ☺ ☺ ☺ ☺

Who Noticed: _____

Who Left The Room: _____

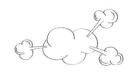

NOTES

NOTES

Date: ___ / ___ / ___   Sun Mon Tue Wed Thu Fri Sat

Time of Fart: _____ am/pm   **Duration:** ___ min ___ sec

Fart Intensity:
- ○ **Gentle Puff** (barely there, quick & unscented)
- ○ **SBD** (silent but deadly)
- ○ **Military March** (series of puffs with mild scent)
- ○ **Classic** (quick, loud, stinky scent but fades quickly)
- ○ **Thunder Rumble** (long, loud & stinky)
- ○ **Diarrhea Storm** (explosive, wet & clears the room)
- ○ **Oh, Crap!** (self explanatory)

Fart Enjoyment Scale: ☺ ☺ ☺ ☺ ☺

Who Noticed: _____

Who Left The Room: _____

Date: ___ / ___ / ___   Sun Mon Tue Wed Thu Fri Sat

Time of Fart: _____ am/pm   **Duration:** ___ min ___ sec

Fart Intensity:
- ○ **Gentle Puff** (barely there, quick & unscented)
- ○ **SBD** (silent but deadly)
- ○ **Military March** (series of puffs with mild scent)
- ○ **Classic** (quick, loud, stinky scent but fades quickly)
- ○ **Thunder Rumble** (long, loud & stinky)
- ○ **Diarrhea Storm** (explosive, wet & clears the room)
- ○ **Oh, Crap!** (self explanatory)

Fart Enjoyment Scale: ☺ ☺ ☺ ☺ ☺

Who Noticed: _____

Who Left The Room: _____

NOTES

NOTES

Date: ___ / ___ / ___ Sun Mon Tue Wed Thu Fri Sat

Time of Fart: _____ am/pm **Duration:** ___ min ___ sec

Fart Intensity:
- ○ **Gentle Puff** (barely there, quick & unscented)
- ○ **SBD** (silent but deadly)
- ○ **Military March** (series of puffs with mild scent)
- ○ **Classic** (quick, loud, stinky scent but fades quickly)
- ○ **Thunder Rumble** (long, loud & stinky)
- ○ **Diarrhea Storm** (explosive, wet & clears the room)
- ○ **Oh, Crap!** (self explanatory)

Fart Enjoyment Scale: ☺ ☺ ☺ ☺ ☺

Who Noticed: _____

Who Left The Room: _____

Date: ___ / ___ / ___ Sun Mon Tue Wed Thu Fri Sat

Time of Fart: _____ am/pm **Duration:** ___ min ___ sec

Fart Intensity:
- ○ **Gentle Puff** (barely there, quick & unscented)
- ○ **SBD** (silent but deadly)
- ○ **Military March** (series of puffs with mild scent)
- ○ **Classic** (quick, loud, stinky scent but fades quickly)
- ○ **Thunder Rumble** (long, loud & stinky)
- ○ **Diarrhea Storm** (explosive, wet & clears the room)
- ○ **Oh, Crap!** (self explanatory)

Fart Enjoyment Scale: ☺ ☺ ☺ ☺ ☺

Who Noticed: _____

Who Left The Room: _____

NOTES

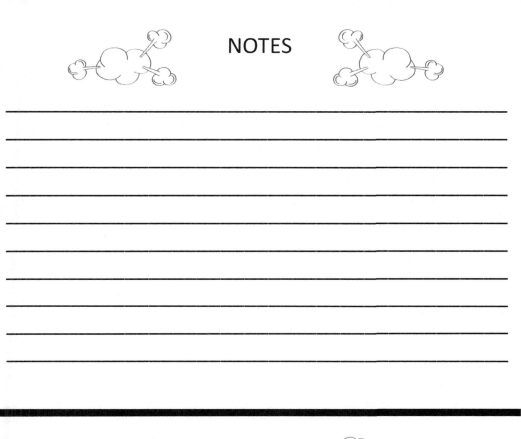

NOTES

Date: ___ / ___ / ___   Sun Mon Tue Wed Thu Fri Sat

Time of Fart: _____ am/pm   **Duration:** ___ min ___ sec

Fart Intensity:
- ○ **Gentle Puff** (barely there, quick & unscented)
- ○ **SBD** (silent but deadly)
- ○ **Military March** (series of puffs with mild scent)
- ○ **Classic** (quick, loud, stinky scent but fades quickly)
- ○ **Thunder Rumble** (long, loud & stinky)
- ○ **Diarrhea Storm** (explosive, wet & clears the room)
- ○ **Oh, Crap!** (self explanatory)

Fart Enjoyment Scale: ☺ ☺ ☺ ☺ ☺

Who Noticed: _____

Who Left The Room: _____

Date: ___ / ___ / ___   Sun Mon Tue Wed Thu Fri Sat

Time of Fart: _____ am/pm   **Duration:** ___ min ___ sec

Fart Intensity:
- ○ **Gentle Puff** (barely there, quick & unscented)
- ○ **SBD** (silent but deadly)
- ○ **Military March** (series of puffs with mild scent)
- ○ **Classic** (quick, loud, stinky scent but fades quickly)
- ○ **Thunder Rumble** (long, loud & stinky)
- ○ **Diarrhea Storm** (explosive, wet & clears the room)
- ○ **Oh, Crap!** (self explanatory)

Fart Enjoyment Scale: ☺ ☺ ☺ ☺ ☺

Who Noticed: _____

Who Left The Room: _____

NOTES

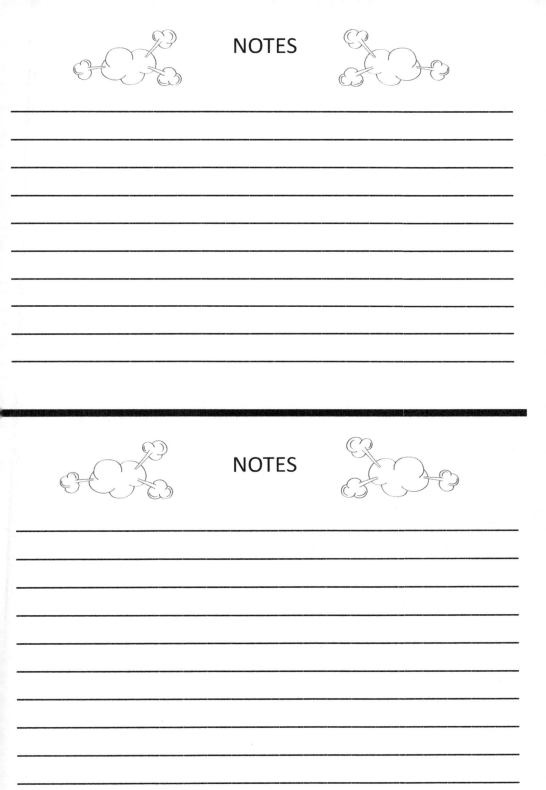

NOTES

Date: ___ / ___ / ___   Sun   Mon   Tue   Wed   Thu   Fri   Sat

Time of Fart: _____ am/pm   **Duration:** ___ min ___ sec

Fart Intensity:
- ○ **Gentle Puff** (barely there, quick & unscented)
- ○ **SBD** (silent but deadly)
- ○ **Military March** (series of puffs with mild scent)
- ○ **Classic** (quick, loud, stinky scent but fades quickly)
- ○ **Thunder Rumble** (long, loud & stinky)
- ○ **Diarrhea Storm** (explosive, wet & clears the room)
- ○ **Oh, Crap!** (self explanatory)

Fart Enjoyment Scale: ☺ ☺ ☺ ☺ ☺

Who Noticed: _____

Who Left The Room: _____

Date: ___ / ___ / ___   Sun   Mon   Tue   Wed   Thu   Fri   Sat

Time of Fart: _____ am/pm   **Duration:** ___ min ___ sec

Fart Intensity:
- ○ **Gentle Puff** (barely there, quick & unscented)
- ○ **SBD** (silent but deadly)
- ○ **Military March** (series of puffs with mild scent)
- ○ **Classic** (quick, loud, stinky scent but fades quickly)
- ○ **Thunder Rumble** (long, loud & stinky)
- ○ **Diarrhea Storm** (explosive, wet & clears the room)
- ○ **Oh, Crap!** (self explanatory)

Fart Enjoyment Scale: ☺ ☺ ☺ ☺ ☺

Who Noticed: _____

Who Left The Room: _____

NOTES

NOTES

Date: ___ / ___ / ___   Sun Mon Tue Wed Thu Fri Sat

Time of Fart: _____ am/pm   **Duration:** ___ min ___ sec

Fart Intensity:
- ○ **Gentle Puff** (barely there, quick & unscented)
- ○ **SBD** (silent but deadly)
- ○ **Military March** (series of puffs with mild scent)
- ○ **Classic** (quick, loud, stinky scent but fades quickly)
- ○ **Thunder Rumble** (long, loud & stinky)
- ○ **Diarrhea Storm** (explosive, wet & clears the room)
- ○ **Oh, Crap!** (self explanatory)

Fart Enjoyment Scale: ☺ ☺ ☺ ☺ ☺

Who Noticed: _____

Who Left The Room: _____

Date: ___ / ___ / ___   Sun Mon Tue Wed Thu Fri Sat

Time of Fart: _____ am/pm   **Duration:** ___ min ___ sec

Fart Intensity:
- ○ **Gentle Puff** (barely there, quick & unscented)
- ○ **SBD** (silent but deadly)
- ○ **Military March** (series of puffs with mild scent)
- ○ **Classic** (quick, loud, stinky scent but fades quickly)
- ○ **Thunder Rumble** (long, loud & stinky)
- ○ **Diarrhea Storm** (explosive, wet & clears the room)
- ○ **Oh, Crap!** (self explanatory)

Fart Enjoyment Scale: ☺ ☺ ☺ ☺ ☺

Who Noticed: _____

Who Left The Room: _____

NOTES

NOTES

Date: ___ / ___ / ___   Sun Mon Tue Wed Thu Fri Sat

Time of Fart: _____ am/pm   **Duration:** ___ min ___ sec

Fart Intensity:
- ○ **Gentle Puff** (barely there, quick & unscented)
- ○ **SBD** (silent but deadly)
- ○ **Military March** (series of puffs with mild scent)
- ○ **Classic** (quick, loud, stinky scent but fades quickly)
- ○ **Thunder Rumble** (long, loud & stinky)
- ○ **Diarrhea Storm** (explosive, wet & clears the room)
- ○ **Oh, Crap!** (self explanatory)

Fart Enjoyment Scale: ☺ ☺ ☺ ☺ ☺

Who Noticed: _____

Who Left The Room: _____

Date: ___ / ___ / ___   Sun Mon Tue Wed Thu Fri Sat

Time of Fart: _____ am/pm   **Duration:** ___ min ___ sec

Fart Intensity:
- ○ **Gentle Puff** (barely there, quick & unscented)
- ○ **SBD** (silent but deadly)
- ○ **Military March** (series of puffs with mild scent)
- ○ **Classic** (quick, loud, stinky scent but fades quickly)
- ○ **Thunder Rumble** (long, loud & stinky)
- ○ **Diarrhea Storm** (explosive, wet & clears the room)
- ○ **Oh, Crap!** (self explanatory)

Fart Enjoyment Scale: ☺ ☺ ☺ ☺ ☺

Who Noticed: _____

Who Left The Room: _____

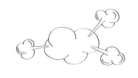
NOTES

NOTES

Date: ___ / ___ / ___   Sun Mon Tue Wed Thu Fri Sat

Time of Fart: _____ am/pm   **Duration:** ___ min ___ sec

Fart Intensity:
- ○ **Gentle Puff** (barely there, quick & unscented)
- ○ **SBD** (silent but deadly)
- ○ **Military March** (series of puffs with mild scent)
- ○ **Classic** (quick, loud, stinky scent but fades quickly)
- ○ **Thunder Rumble** (long, loud & stinky)
- ○ **Diarrhea Storm** (explosive, wet & clears the room)
- ○ **Oh, Crap!** (self explanatory)

Fart Enjoyment Scale: ☺ ☺ ☺ ☺ ☺

Who Noticed: _____

Who Left The Room: _____

Date: ___ / ___ / ___   Sun Mon Tue Wed Thu Fri Sat

Time of Fart: _____ am/pm   **Duration:** ___ min ___ sec

Fart Intensity:
- ○ **Gentle Puff** (barely there, quick & unscented)
- ○ **SBD** (silent but deadly)
- ○ **Military March** (series of puffs with mild scent)
- ○ **Classic** (quick, loud, stinky scent but fades quickly)
- ○ **Thunder Rumble** (long, loud & stinky)
- ○ **Diarrhea Storm** (explosive, wet & clears the room)
- ○ **Oh, Crap!** (self explanatory)

Fart Enjoyment Scale: ☺ ☺ ☺ ☺ ☺

Who Noticed: _____

Who Left The Room: _____

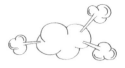

NOTES

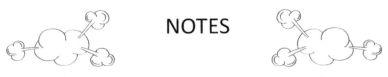

NOTES

Date: ___ / ___ / ___   Sun Mon Tue Wed Thu Fri Sat

Time of Fart: _____ am/pm   **Duration:** ___ min ___ sec

Fart Intensity:
- ○ **Gentle Puff** (barely there, quick & unscented)
- ○ **SBD** (silent but deadly)
- ○ **Military March** (series of puffs with mild scent)
- ○ **Classic** (quick, loud, stinky scent but fades quickly)
- ○ **Thunder Rumble** (long, loud & stinky)
- ○ **Diarrhea Storm** (explosive, wet & clears the room)
- ○ **Oh, Crap!** (self explanatory)

Fart Enjoyment Scale: ☺ ☺ ☺ ☺ ☺

Who Noticed: _____

Who Left The Room: _____

Date: ___ / ___ / ___   Sun Mon Tue Wed Thu Fri Sat

Time of Fart: _____ am/pm   **Duration:** ___ min ___ sec

Fart Intensity:
- ○ **Gentle Puff** (barely there, quick & unscented)
- ○ **SBD** (silent but deadly)
- ○ **Military March** (series of puffs with mild scent)
- ○ **Classic** (quick, loud, stinky scent but fades quickly)
- ○ **Thunder Rumble** (long, loud & stinky)
- ○ **Diarrhea Storm** (explosive, wet & clears the room)
- ○ **Oh, Crap!** (self explanatory)

Fart Enjoyment Scale: ☺ ☺ ☺ ☺ ☺

Who Noticed: _____

Who Left The Room: _____

NOTES

_____
_____
_____
_____
_____
_____
_____
_____
_____
_____

NOTES

_____
_____
_____
_____
_____
_____
_____
_____
_____

Date: ___ / ___ / ___ Sun Mon Tue Wed Thu Fri Sat

Time of Fart: _____ am/pm **Duration:** ___ min ___ sec

Fart Intensity:
- ○ **Gentle Puff** (barely there, quick & unscented)
- ○ **SBD** (silent but deadly)
- ○ **Military March** (series of puffs with mild scent)
- ○ **Classic** (quick, loud, stinky scent but fades quickly)
- ○ **Thunder Rumble** (long, loud & stinky)
- ○ **Diarrhea Storm** (explosive, wet & clears the room)
- ○ **Oh, Crap!** (self explanatory)

Fart Enjoyment Scale: ☺ ☺ ☺ ☺ ☺

Who Noticed: _____

Who Left The Room: _____

Date: ___ / ___ / ___ Sun Mon Tue Wed Thu Fri Sat

Time of Fart: _____ am/pm **Duration:** ___ min ___ sec

Fart Intensity:
- ○ **Gentle Puff** (barely there, quick & unscented)
- ○ **SBD** (silent but deadly)
- ○ **Military March** (series of puffs with mild scent)
- ○ **Classic** (quick, loud, stinky scent but fades quickly)
- ○ **Thunder Rumble** (long, loud & stinky)
- ○ **Diarrhea Storm** (explosive, wet & clears the room)
- ○ **Oh, Crap!** (self explanatory)

Fart Enjoyment Scale: ☺ ☺ ☺ ☺ ☺

Who Noticed: _____

Who Left The Room: _____

Printed in Great Britain
by Amazon

31684650R00056